The Writing Prompts Workbook, Grades 3-4:
Story Starters for Journals, Assignments and More

Bryan Cohen

Edited by Debra Cohen and Amy Crater.

ISBN: 0985482214
ISBN-13: 978-0-9854822-1-3

DEDICATION

I dedicate this book to Miss Adler, who taught me that planning ahead would allow me to accomplish anything.

CONTENTS

INTRODUCTION

Welcome to *The Writing Prompts Workbook*! Within these pages you'll find 200 writing prompts, two on each page, that will help to stimulate the imagination of your students or children. I've found that the key to allowing students to fully latch onto an idea is to give them a scenario followed by a question. In answering the question, young writers can take the same prompt a million different directions. You may even want to try photocopying a page and have your writers take on the same prompt at the beginning and the end of a school year just to see how different their storytelling has become.

The Writing Prompts Workbook series is a collection of books I've created after seeing how many parents and teachers have visited my website, Build Creative Writing Ideas (located at http://www.build-creative-writing-ideas.com). I have adapted my thousands of prompts into six workbooks designed to take a first grader creatively all the way up through the end of high school. The six books are available for grades 1-2, 3-4, 5-6, 7-8, 9-10 and 11-12. The prompts become more complex with each volume, but continue to remain imaginative and creative throughout.

I love hearing about the progress of students on my site and I'm always interested in hearing new ideas for delivering creative writing prompts to writers from the ages of five to 105. Feel free to contact me on my website for any questions and comments you can think of. I hope you and your future best-selling authors thoroughly enjoy this and future books in the series. Happy writing!

Sincerely,
Bryan Cohen
Author of *The Writing Prompts Workbook* Series

PS: While there is space below each prompt for your budding writers to write, there is a good chance they may have more to say than they can fit on the page. There is an extra lined page in the back if you'd like to photocopy it, but I strongly suggest that you also get a notebook and some extra pencils just in case. A dictionary for words they don't know yet may also be helpful.

Name _____ Date _____

1. What is the best book that you've ever read? Who are some of the characters from it and what makes you like them so much? What makes this book so special to you?

_____

_____

_____

_____

2. What are a few of the things that you like about reading? What are some of the things that you don't like about reading? What would you do to improve upon some of the things that you don't enjoy so much?

_____

_____

_____

_____

Name _____ Date _____

3. What is the worst book you've ever read? Why didn't you like it?
Imagine that you had to meet with the person who wrote the book (the author). What would you say to him or her about the book?

_____

_____

_____

_____

_____

4. Which do you like better, reading out loud in a group or reading silently and alone? Discuss the positives and the negatives of both and how you might learn differently with each method.

_____

_____

_____

_____

_____

Name _____ Date _____

5. Have your parents ever read you a bedtime story? Did they read to you from a book or did they make up a story on the spot? Which one was your favorite and why? If your parents never read you a bedtime story, make one up that you might have enjoyed when you were really little.

_____

_____

_____

_____

_____

6. What about reading is difficult for you and what about reading is easy for you? How do you think you could work on the tough things to become a better reader? Keep in mind that you can learn anything if you give it enough time and effort.

_____

_____

_____

_____

Name _____ Date _____

7. What is the strangest thing you've ever read? Was it from a book, a magazine or online? How did you feel when you read these weird words and what did you do after reading it?

_____

_____

_____

_____

_____

8. Have you ever read something that changed your life? For example, you read something that taught you something new or that made you think about a certain subject in a new way? If so, talk about it in detail. If not, write something down that might change the life of someone you know in a good way.

_____

_____

_____

_____

_____

Name _____ Date _____

9. Have you ever read the lyrics of a song? It can be a lot different
from listening to the song on your computer, iPod or the radio. How is it different and
why?

_____

_____

_____

_____

10. Describe how your reading skills help you with the following areas: nutrition labels,
instructions for toys, traffic signs, baking recipes (like cookies) and "sale" signs at the
mall.

_____

_____

_____

_____

Name _____ Date _____

11. Your body is made up of millions of tiny cells that help to make sure your body functions properly. If your cells could talk about you, what do you think they would say? Would they say you're a pretty good person? That you eat right and exercise? Go into extreme detail.

_____

_____

_____

_____

_____

12. Biology is the study of life and all living things in the world. Have you ever gotten a chance to look at some crazy life forms other than insects, pets and humans? What are some of these living things you've seen and what have they taught you about biology?

_____

_____

_____

_____

_____

Name _____ Date _____

13. One of the major areas of science is chemistry. Describe how chemistry is a part of the following items in your life: food, toothpaste, clothing, medicine and soap.

_____

_____

_____

_____

_____

14. Physics is the science that studies how things move through the world. Some examples of things that involve physics are a car moving down the road, a baseball being hit through the air by a bat and an egg falling off the counter and onto the ground. What are some examples of physics in your life?

_____

_____

_____

_____

_____

Name _____ Date _____

15. What are at least five things that you like about science and
scientific experiments? How would you explain the good things about science to a person
who hates the subject?

_____

_____

_____

_____

_____

16. Over the next decade or so, you will learn how lots of different things in your body
work, like your brain, heart and teeth. Since you might not know all of these things yet,
how would you guess that the brain works? How do you think the heart works? How do
teeth work?

_____

_____

_____

_____

Name _____ Date _____

17. Many people believe that in the future (the next 20 to 50 years)
lots of things will change about science and technology like flying cars and robot friends.
How do you think the science of the world will change in the next 20 to 50 years? Go into
extreme detail.

_____

_____

_____

_____

18. One of the interesting subjects of scientific study is astronomy, the study of stars,
planets, galaxies and more. Imagine that you and your classmates are out on an astronomy
field trip, looking at the stars. Something amazing happens. What is it and what do you all
do about it?

_____

_____

_____

_____

Name _____ Date _____

19. Millions of years ago, the surfaces of the earth used to be shaped differently with all of the continents stuck together with all the oceans around the outside like one giant island. What do you think happened to make all of the land split up into the seven continents we have today?

_____

_____

_____

_____

20. Of the types of science we've mentioned, like biology, chemistry, physics and astronomy, which do you find the most interesting and why?

_____

_____

_____

_____

Name _____ Date _____

21. Imagine that you have sat down for a math test and after looking
at the problems you realize you accidentally studied for the wrong chapter! The questions
almost look like a foreign language! What could you do and how do you deal with this
tough situation?

_____

_____

_____

_____

_____

22. What is the part of math that you like the most? What is the part that you like the least?
What are at least three ways you might be able to get the part you like the least to be more
interesting, exciting and fun?

_____

_____

_____

_____

Name _____ Date _____

23. What do you do when you have difficulty understanding a certain concept in math? Do you ask your teacher for help? Do you talk with your parents? Do you figure it out yourself? Write a little story about you tackling a tough math problem or lesson.

_____

_____

_____

_____

_____

24. What are some ways that you use math in the real world? Talk about at least five different ways you have used math just in the last month.

_____

_____

_____

_____

Name _____ Date _____

25. One important way we use math is for keeping track of our money. How do you personally keep track of your money? Do you use a piggy bank? Do you get an allowance? List five ways that you can save or earn money and discuss how your math skills help you to manage your money.

_____

_____

_____

_____

_____

26. Are your parents more math people or writing people? Have you ever been able to stump your parents with a tough math problem? If not, write a little story in which you come up with a math riddle to confuse your parents.

_____

_____

_____

_____

Name _____ Date _____

27. Another way we use math is to keep up with scores in our favorite sports like football and baseball. How do we use math to help us understand what's going on in those exciting games? What kind of math do the players and coaches have to use during the games?

_____

_____

_____

_____

_____

28. Describe how each of the following real world professions might have to use math in their everyday jobs: scientist, firefighter, policeman, teacher and engineer.

_____

_____

_____

_____

_____

Name _____ Date _____

29. Talk about how even those in non-mathematics related jobs have
to use math every so often: painter, poet, musician, dancer, newspaper reporter.

_____

_____

_____

_____

30. How is math used in the following areas that you might enjoy: roller coasters,
swimming pools, video games, television and candy bars.

_____

_____

_____

_____

Name _____ Date _____

31. What kind of lunch do you usually eat during school? Do you
buy lunch or does someone pack your lunch for you? What are all of the standard foods
that you eat and what would you change about it if you had a chance?

_____

_____

_____

_____

32. Who are the people that you typically sit with during lunch time? Describe all of them,
what they typically eat and what you think they bring to the table. For example, somebody
who tells a lot of jokes is a good addition to the table because he makes lunch a fun time.

_____

_____

_____

_____

Name _____ Date _____

33. Imagine that during lunch a crazy food fight has broken out and
you have hidden under a table to avoid getting hit with pizza and burgers. What happens
next?

_____

_____

_____

_____

34. What is the wackiest lunch you've ever had at school? Did your mom try to spice
things up with some confusing sandwich choices? Did you trade the things in your lunch
bag for something wild and crazy? If you've never had a crazy lunch, make up a story in
which you end up with an unusual lunch due to strange circumstances.

_____

_____

_____

_____

Name _____ Date _____

35. Imagine that there is a cute boy or girl that you want to sit with
and talk to across the lunch room. Tell the story of how you work up the nerve to do it and
what you two talk about.

_____

_____

_____

_____

_____

36. If you could create the perfect lunch for yourself, from anywhere in the world, what
would you have in your lunch bag? Go into extreme detail and tell the story of how jealous
your lunch buddies would be.

_____

_____

_____

_____

_____

Name _____ Date _____

37. What do you and your lunch friends typically talk about at the
lunch table? Write a little dialogue that shows what you usually discuss. If you usually just
eat, make up a story in which you talk about something very important.

_____

_____

_____

_____

_____

38. If a person in the lunch room fell down and their food went everywhere, what would
you do and why? Now imagine that it was you who fell down, what would you hope that
other people would do?

_____

_____

_____

_____

Name _____ Date _____

39. What do you think school lunches are like in other schools?

What about in other countries? There are no right answers or wrong answers here, just imagine what some of the differences might be and write about what it'd be like to go there for a lunch visit.

_____

_____

_____

_____

_____

40. One of your friends has had 20 pizzas delivered to the lunch room for everyone to share. When the pizza delivery guy arrives he asks, "Alright, who is paying?" What do you and your friends do?

_____

_____

_____

_____

Name _____ Date _____

41. Who is your favorite movie or television actor? Imagine that you get to spend a day with this person and you have to report back to the class about your time together. What do you say during your presentation?

_____

_____

_____

_____

42. If you could be a part of any television show or movie, what would it be and why? What part would you play? Write about a day in the life of filming the show or movie.

_____

_____

_____

_____

Name _____ Date _____

43. The television networks have come knocking on your door asking you to write the next great comedy or drama. What do you make your show about and who are some of the actors you would cast in it?

_____

_____

_____

_____

44. A movie crew has asked your family if they can use the house for a major action blockbuster. Your parents said, "Yes!" and now you get to see all the behind-the-scenes action. What do you see, who do you meet and what do you learn during the process?

_____

_____

_____

_____

Name _____ Date _____

45. After an amazing series of events, you star in a movie and you get nominated for an Academy Award, the most prestigious honor an actor can get! At the ceremony, the Academy picks you as the winner! Now you have to go up on stage and give a speech. What would you say during your speech? Who would you thank?

_____

_____

_____

_____

46. You have become the network executive for NBC, one of the main television stations. They have given you the choice of what shows you want to put on every night of the week. What shows do you pick and what new ones do you create from scratch?

_____

_____

_____

_____

Name _____ Date _____

47. How are movies and television different from real life? What are
some imaginary things that happen on television and the movies that never happen in
reality?

_____

_____

_____

_____

_____

48. If you could pick one character to be your movie boyfriend or girlfriend, who would it
be? What would it be like to share a smooch on screen with him or her?

_____

_____

_____

_____

Name _____ Date _____

49. Right now, a big thing in technology is 3D (three dimensional) televisions and movie screens. What do you think will be the next step in entertainment technology? What about 4D or Smell-o-Vision? Come up with an idea and pitch your case on why it would be amazing.

_____

_____

_____

_____

50. You wake up one morning and see a camera out of the corner of your eye. It turns out that you and your family are going to be part of a reality show on a major television network. How does your life change now that there is always a camera wherever you turn? Would you like to be in this situation? Why or why not?

_____

_____

_____

_____

Name _____ Date _____

51. What kind of video game systems do you and your family have inside your house? Tell the story of how you got each of them. If you don't have any video game systems, create a story of how your family might get one in the future.

_____

_____

_____

_____

_____

52. What is your favorite video game that you've ever played and what system was it for? Write a story about a day in which you had a particularly great time playing it.

_____

_____

_____

_____

_____

Name _____ Date _____

53. What do you think are some of the benefits of video games?

What are some of the reasons you think kids maybe shouldn't play video games? Do the pros outweigh the cons or do you think video games are a bad thing for kids?

_____

_____

_____

_____

54. Some people think that video games keep kids from going outside and getting exercise as much as before video games existed. Do you agree or disagree and why?

_____

_____

_____

_____

Name _____ Date _____

55. The recent video game systems like Xbox360 and Wii are a lot
of fun and they have amazing graphics. What do you think the video game systems of the
future will be like? What new features might they have and what kind of games will they
provide?

_____

_____

_____

_____

_____

56. The first video games were really simple and you could only do a couple of things like
bounce a ball from one side of the screen to the other. If you went back in time to those
days, do you think you would enjoy such simple games?

_____

_____

_____

_____

_____

Name _____ Date _____

57. Have you ever played a video game that your parents told you
that you weren't allowed to play? Perhaps it had excessive violence or bad language. What
was the game like? Do you understand why your parents might not want you to play it?

_____

_____

_____

_____

_____

58. If you could be a character inside any video game, which one would it be and why?
Tell a story about a day in the life for your new video game character.

_____

_____

_____

_____

Name _____ Date _____

59. Imagine that you are a game developer for the company that makes some of the biggest games today. You need to come up with an amazing idea that everyone will like. What is the idea? Tell the story of its amazing success in the marketplace.

_____

_____

_____

_____

60. Many video games are catered toward boys, leading girls to often leave video games alone. If you could create a video game that was for girls only, what would it be? Do you think boys might want to try it too?

_____

_____

_____

_____

Name _____ Date _____

61. What are your three favorite sports? Why do you like them, why do you play them and why do you watch them?

_____

_____

_____

_____

62. If you could be any athlete in the world, who would you be and why? Describe a typical day for you as this super athlete person.

_____

_____

_____

_____

Name _____ Date _____

63. Have you ever had an amazing athletic moment of success? Like scoring a goal in soccer or getting a hit in baseball? If so, describe the lead up to that moment and how it felt afterwards. If not, create a story of you doing something incredible during a sporting event.

_____

_____

_____

_____

64. What does it mean for you to be on an athletic team? You all have a team name, the same team colors and you meet together multiple times a week. Do you have a special bond with these people or is it just dumb luck that has you all together?

_____

_____

_____

_____

Name _____ Date _____

65. How does participating in sports change you? Do you think that you've learned anything from being involved in athletics and why or why not? Have you kept in better shape as a result?

_____

_____

_____

_____

66. Are there some sports that you don't like? Why don't you like them and why don't you enjoy either playing them or watching them? What could you change about the sport that would make it more fun for you?

_____

_____

_____

_____

Name _____ Date _____

67. Create your own sport from scratch. Give it your own rules, your own uniforms and your own name. Make sure to create a sport that you and all your friends would want to play!

_____

_____

_____

_____

_____

68. During gym class or physical education class, you and your classmates get the opportunity to play sports and learn about athletics. What is your favorite part about this class? What is your least favorite part? If you had the choice would you have more of this class, less of it, or the same amount?

_____

_____

_____

_____

_____

Name _____ Date _____

69. Imagine 15 years down the line, you have become a professional athlete at your particular sport. You're either in the NBA, the NFL, the NHL or some other worldwide organization in which you get paid to play sports. What is it like? What team do you play for? Do you have a lot of fans? Go into extreme detail.

_____

_____

_____

_____

70. Some people say that playing sports is good for your brain and your overall health. What are some of the benefits that you get from sports? Does it make you feel happier? Does it help you make new friends?

_____

_____

_____

_____

Name _____ Date _____

71. If you could live at any time in history, when would it be and
what would you do there? Would it be the time of the dinosaurs or the Wild West? Maybe
it would be the days of American Revolution. If you can't pick just one, feel free to write
about a few.

_____

_____

_____

_____

_____

72. You have been given a magical amulet that gives you and only you 48 hours in a day
instead of just 24. This gives you time to do twice as many things in one day! What will
you do with your new amount of time?

_____

_____

_____

_____

Name _____ Date _____

73. What is your favorite time of the day and why? Is it right when
you get up in the morning? Is it lunchtime? What do you do during that time that makes
you enjoy it so much?

_____

_____

_____

_____

74. If you had a choice to be any age, what would it be and why? What are some of the
things you could do at that age that you can't do now (unless you pick the age you are, then
say what some of the things are you can do now)?

_____

_____

_____

_____

Name _____ Date _____

75. They say that time flies when you're having fun. Do you agree
that time goes by faster when you're having a good time and that it goes by slower when
you're not? Give an example of each situation from your own life.

_____

_____

_____

_____

76. H.G. Wells has arrived at your door with a time machine! It seems that someone has
been trying to change the past so that ice cream never gets made and he wants you to come
along and help. Detail your adventures of trying to stop this dastardly criminal.

_____

_____

_____

_____

Name _____ Date _____

77. What would you do if you could teleport to any place in the world just by thinking it? Where would you go and why?

_____

_____

_____

_____

78. There are lots of other planets in the universe other than Earth and scientists think that there might be other life on one of them. Do you think that there are other life forms than those on Earth and if so, what are they like and where do they live?

_____

_____

_____

_____

Name _____ Date _____

79. You have been selected for the kid mission to Mars! Go into extreme detail about the training process, the space shuttle ride to the planet and what it's like being on the surface of the Martian planet.

_____

_____

_____

_____

_____

80. You wake up to realize that it's Tuesday … even though it was Tuesday yesterday! You relive the same day, with the same things happening and when you go to sleep … it's Tuesday again when you wake up! What do you do as you keep reliving the same day over and over?

_____

_____

_____

_____

_____

Name _____ Date _____

81. Some kids have lessons for certain musical instruments like the piano or the clarinet. Have you ever learned a musical instrument? If so, what was it like and what did you learn from it? If not, imagine that you get the chance to learn your favorite instrument. What is it like and how do you feel playing it?

_____

_____

_____

_____

82. What kind of music do you like listening to outside of school? Do you enjoy listening to what your parents listen to or is their taste in music not for you? If you had the choice to pick music to play during school, what would it be?

_____

_____

_____

_____

Name _____ Date _____

83. The school play has started casting its actors ... and you are going to be the star of the show! What is the play (you can make one up) and how do you deal with the following things: learning your lines, trying on your costumes, working with the other actors, taking direction and a hefty dose of stage fright on opening night?

_____

_____

_____

_____

_____

84. In nearly all of the television shows and movies you watch, there are hundreds of actors and technical people working to entertain you. Which of the following positions would you rather be and why: actor, writer, director, sound technician, light technician or producer?

_____

_____

_____

_____

_____

Name _____ Date _____

85. Whether you only do art during class in school, or if you take a painting, drawing or ceramics class outside of school, art can be a relaxing and challenging activity. How do you feel when you're doing art? What do you think it means to be a talented artist? Would you do more or less art if you had a choice?

_____

_____

_____

_____

86. Have you ever been to a museum? These are amazing places that are full of art and history from hundreds (or thousands) of years ago until today. Some kids find museums boring while others find them full of interesting items. What would you (or do you) think of a room full of art and history? If you find it boring, what would you do to change it? If you find it exciting, what do you like about it the most?

_____

_____

_____

_____

Name _____ Date _____

87. There are many different kinds of dance that kids and adults can learn. Some dances are for particular cultures like Irish dancing and others are for everyone like ballroom dancing. Have you ever learned a dance? If so, what was it like trying to learn the right steps to the beat of the music? If not, imagine that you had to learn a dance to show your whole class and tell a little story about it.

_____

_____

_____

_____

88. One of the ways to combine athletics and art is called martial arts. This includes different types like karate, tae kwon do and judo. Have you ever practiced martial arts? If so, what was it like and what did you learn about yourself during your lessons? If not, create a story in which you are a master martial artist, teaching a certain form to your students.

_____

_____

_____

_____

Name _____ Date _____

89. Who is your favorite singer and why? Have you ever dreamed of become a famous singer yourself? What would a day in your fabulous singing life be like?

_____

_____

_____

_____

90. Are there are artistic activities that you participate in that aren't in the list of music, theatre, art, dance, martial arts and singing? If so, tell a little bit about it here. If not, make up a new form of art and tell us why it's artistic and fun.

_____

_____

_____

_____

Name _____ Date _____

91. What is your favorite type of writing? Do you like writing in journals, writing songs, writing poetry, writing essays or some other type? Why do you like it and how do you feel when you write like that?

_____

_____

_____

_____

_____

92. If you could write a book during your spare time outside of school, what would it be about and why? Imagine that you have sold the book to a big publisher and you're going to tour around the world with it. What would you say about the book to your legions of fans?

_____

_____

_____

_____

_____

Name _____ Date _____

93. Have you ever taken a class on writing outside of school? If so, what did you learn about writing and what did you write during it? If not, what do you think you might learn about writing in a non-academic setting? Would you learn how to write the next Harry Potter book?

_____

_____

_____

_____

94. Two of the major types of writing are fiction and non-fiction. Fiction is made up and non-fiction is about things that definitely happened. If you had the choice, would you write fiction or non-fiction? What would a few of your book titles be?

_____

_____

_____

_____

Name _____ Date _____

95. Have you ever had to write a poem? There are many different types of poems. Some can rhyme, some don't rhyme at all. Some are short and some are as long as a whole book. Write a poem about whatever you feel like. It doesn't need to rhyme or make sense, just try to express a feeling or two using the words and see what you come up with.

_____

_____

_____

_____

_____

96. Another type of writing is to write a script for a play or a movie. If you could create a play or movie what would it be called and what would it be about? Write at least two scenes from the play or movie with multiple characters. Make sure it's something that you'd want to watch!

_____

_____

_____

_____

_____

Name _____ Date _____

97. What's the most interesting thing that you've ever read inside or
outside of class? Why was it so memorable? Did you learn something new? Did it prove
something you'd previously believed wrong? How hard do you think it would be for you to
write something with just as much impact?

_____

_____

_____

_____

98. Some of the most popular writers in the world are song writers. They come up with the
lyrics that your favorite singers turn into #1 hits or that they use in popular musicals. Write
a short song on whatever subject you choose. Don't worry about the music behind it, just
write the song and see how it turns out.

_____

_____

_____

_____

Name _____ Date _____

99. Before the written word existed (on paper and on computers)
certain cultures had no way of writing their stories down, so they passed down the stories
to each other through oral communication What is a story that you have heard that you
would pass down to future generations? Write the story here. Why is this story the tale that
you have chosen?

_____

_____

_____

_____

_____

100. A folktale is often a story of somewhat magical creatures that teaches the reader a
lesson in the end. Write your own folktale based on some of the lessons you've learned in
your own lifetime.

_____

_____

_____

_____

_____

Name _____ Date _____

101. Who is your favorite famous person? What do you like about
him or her and would you like to do what he or she does when you grow up? Why?

_____

_____

_____

_____

102. If you could be a character in any book or movie who would it be? What would you
do differently and what would you do the same as the character? Why?

_____

_____

_____

_____

Name _____ Date _____

103. What is your favorite thing to do during the summer? Is it camp? Taking a vacation? Hanging out in the house? Why do you like it so much?

_____

_____

_____

_____

104. What do you think your parents were like when they were your age? Do you think they were the same as you or different from you? Would you and your parents have been friends?

_____

_____

_____

_____

Name _____ Date _____

105. What is the scariest thing that's ever happened to you? Why was it so scary and how did you deal with it?

_____

_____

_____

_____

106. How big is your family? Talk a little bit about everybody from your family: brothers, sisters, grandparents, cousins, uncles. Talk about everybody!

_____

_____

_____

_____

Name _____ Date _____

107. What is your favorite subject in school? Do you like reading the most? Is it Math or Science? Talk about that subject and why you like it so much.

_____

_____

_____

_____

108. Talk about a fun thing you did with your friends or family. Write about the day from the time you woke up to the time you went to sleep. What did you like so much about it?

_____

_____

_____

_____

Name _____ Date _____

109. What do you think is the best way to help out in your town?
How could you make things better for everybody else? Write about how even one person can make a difference.

_____

_____

_____

_____

_____

110. If you had to write a book what would it be about? Talk about some of the characters from the book and what they would be doing.

_____

_____

_____

_____

Name _____ Date _____

111. If something is interdependent, it means that if a situation affects one part of it, it affects the rest of it. Just like in the food chain, if all of one animal dies out, if affects all the other animals. How do you think the world is interdependent? How do things that happen in your town, state or country affect the rest of the world?

_____

_____

_____

_____

_____

112. Look at the back of a cereal box or a pencil and you will see that it was typically made somewhere other than your home town. If you went to the factory where the items were made, you'd find that they got their raw materials from somewhere else, even possibly from another country. Make up a story in which you track how something is made from beginning to end including all the people who worked on it.

_____

_____

_____

_____

_____

Name _____ Date _____

113. There are a lot of countries in the world that are in conflict with one another. Sometimes this conflict can even lead to war. What do you think are the issues between some of these countries? Why can't they get along?

_____

_____

_____

_____

114. Nowadays, it takes only seconds to get in touch with someone halfway across the globe. Before there were international telephones and the Internet, it could take much longer to talk to people in other countries. How do you think these advances in communication have affected how countries work together?

_____

_____

_____

_____

Name _____ Date _____

115. How do you find out about things going on in the world? Do
your parents tell you? Do you watch the news on television or online? Go into detail about
how you find out about the world. If you don't really know what's going on in the world,
write down a few ways you might be able to improve your world awareness.

_____

_____

_____

_____

116. Some people decide to join the Armed Forces, which means that they may travel
around the world to protect their country. Do you know anybody who is in the Army,
Navy, Air Force or another group? If so, who is it and what do you think it's like for them?
If not, create a story in which you join one of these groups and travel around the world to
protect your country.

_____

_____

_____

_____

Name _____ Date _____

117. In college, one of the things you may be able to do is to "study abroad" which means you can go to a foreign country, take some classes there and learn about the culture for half a year or an entire year. What are a few of the countries you think you might want to go to? What would you want to learn while you're there?

_____

_____

_____

_____

_____

118. In other parts of the world, there are a lot of positive and negative things that you might not have in your life here. For example, in Germany there are many well-crafted and tasty chocolates. In addition, in some parts of the world, there are many tropical diseases that make a lot of people sick. What are some of the positives and negatives of living where you live as opposed to the rest of the world?

_____

_____

_____

_____

_____

Name _____ Date _____

119. People in your class or generally in your life tend to look different based on where their families are from in the world. Do you know where your family is from originally? If so, go into as much detail as possible. If not, imagine the country your relatives came from and how your family ended up where they are today.

_____

_____

_____

_____

120. There are many different animals that live in different parts of the world, depending on how warm or cold the weather is in a particular place. What are some of the animals that you would never find in your backyard? Why do you think they would never live near you?

_____

_____

_____

_____

Name _____ Date _____

121. One of the big problems of bullying is that bullies will make
fun of every way that you are different from what they consider "normal" people. List five
reasons why it's awesome to be different. This would be a way to make the next time
someone makes fun of you a compliment and not an insult.

_____

_____

_____

_____

122. Even though it doesn't seem like it, people who say mean things and bully other kids,
actually tend to feel bad about themselves. This is the main reason that the bullies act the
way they do. Think of a bully in your life or make up a bully and come up with a few
reasons the person might be having a tough time.

_____

_____

_____

_____

Name _____ Date _____

123. Imagine that you have decided to become an "anti-bully," a person who says nice things to build people up instead of mean things to beat people down. Pick three random people in the room and think of a few nice things that you could say to them to build up their self-esteem.

_____

_____

_____

_____

124. Think about a time where you said something mean, or where you didn't stop a mean thing from happening to another kid. How could you have acted differently to make the situation better?

_____

_____

_____

_____

Name _____ Date _____

125. Create a story about a bully who decides to change his ways.
Determine what it is that made the bully want to change and detail how his life is different after switching "mean" to "serene."

_____

_____

_____

_____

_____

126. One of the reasons that people are mean is in an effort to be more popular. Imagine that popularity was completely different and it was based on how nice kids could be to one another. If that were to happen, who would be the popular kids in your school? If the meanest people were the least popular, who would be the least popular kids?

_____

_____

_____

_____

Name _____ Date _____

127. Instead of singling out people and making them feel bad (one term for that is called "ostracizing" a person) we should celebrate our differences and learn things from people that are different from us. Think of a few people in your school who are different who you might be able to learn something from and write a little story about meeting with them.

_____

_____

_____

_____

_____

128. Making a joke at a person's expense is one way of being mean. An example of this is saying that someone is weird or that they look funny so that your friends will laugh. This makes the person feel bad. Try to come up with a few jokes you could use in a situation that wouldn't make anybody feel bad, but would include everybody in the enjoyment.

_____

_____

_____

_____

_____

Name _____ Date _____

129. It is not a good idea to fight a bully with your fists and if the bully has a lot of friends and you're all alone, you might get into serious trouble. What are five things you could do in this situation to stand up for yourself without violence?

_____

_____

_____

_____

130. Becoming a nicer, happier person is not like flipping a light switch. There are certain things you may have to learn in order to stop yourself from being a full-time or part-time bully. What are some of the traits you think you might have to learn and how would you learn them?

_____

_____

_____

_____

Name _____ Date _____

131. Writers have referred to nature as "the great outdoors." Why do
you think they've talked about it like that? What are some of the things that make nature
"great?"

_____

_____

_____

_____

132. One author, Henry David Thoreau, stayed out in nature for a long time and wrote a
book about his experiences being there. Imagine that you were spending a year or two out
in nature. How would you live there? What are the things you would miss about living in
your house? What are the things you wouldn't miss?

_____

_____

_____

_____

Name _____ Date _____

133. In movies like Cinderella, a whistle and a song bring on dozens
of little animal friends to help out the main character. What would your life be like if you
had friends throughout the forest to help you on your way? Which animals would they be
and how would you become friends?

_____

_____

_____

_____

_____

134. There are lots of potential threats to the environment like pollution and deforestation.
Some people even believe that the environment will be damaged beyond repair for your
generation. What will you do to keep the environment safe for you and future generations?

_____

_____

_____

_____

Name _____ Date _____

135. Talk about a time in which you and your friends or you and your family went out into nature. What did you see? What did you learn?

_____

_____

_____

_____

136. Imagine that you, your family and your friends all went into nature to hike up a big mountain. Who would be there and what would their reaction be to the hard work and beautiful scenery? How often would you do this sort of thing if you had a choice?

_____

_____

_____

_____

Name _____ Date _____

137. Have you ever been to the ocean? If so, what were your feelings
the first time you saw that vast body of water? If not, create a story in which you see the
ocean and play around on the beach for the first time.

_____

_____

_____

_____

_____

138. In your lifetime, what are some of the more exotic natural locations you want to go?
Would you want to visit the rainforest or the Arctic Circle? List at least five different
natural habitats. Pick one and then write a story about your trip there.

_____

_____

_____

_____

_____

Name _____ Date _____

139. Pick your favorite animal that lives out in the wild. Create a
story in which you become that animal for a day and have to figure out how to survive in
nature. Write about what you eat, what you do and what other animals you hang out with.

_____

_____

_____

_____

_____

140. Some people believe that nature has become less important for us as technology has
become more advanced. Do you think nature is still important to you and the future
generations? Why do you believe that?

_____

_____

_____

_____

Name _____ Date _____

141. While searching through the attic, you find a giant box with pictures and various items from your parents' past. This includes yearbook photos, wedding stuff and baby pictures of you. What might be some of the surprises you find while snooping around?

_____

_____

_____

_____

142. One day as you are walking around in the school you notice a strange, dusty, old paper hanging from the ceiling. You knock it down and find out that it is a treasure map with a treasure located somewhere in the school. Write a story about how you put together a team of your friends in an effort to find the treasure first!

_____

_____

_____

_____

Name _____ Date _____

143. Lucid dreaming is what happens when you are in a dream, you realize that you are in a dream and yet you don't wake up. This gives you some control over the dream to make it whatever you want it to be. Imagine you started lucid dreaming. What would you do in the dream now that you have full control over it?

_____

_____

_____

_____

144. Life can be very different depending on what career choice your parents have made. Pick one of the following jobs and write about how your life would change if one of your parents worked as any of these: astronaut, professional football player, secret agent, farmer, movie star.

_____

_____

_____

_____

Name _____ Date _____

145. Imagine that you had the ability to plant a garden with whatever plants you wanted. Which plants would you put in your garden and where would the garden be? Would you put any non-plants in the garden as a decoration? How often would you need to take care of it?

_____

_____

_____

_____

_____

146. When you get to high school and college, there are a lot more after-school clubs and activities like French Club, Environmental Club, Volleyball Club, etc. Which clubs do you think you will be most likely to participate in? Why would you pick those clubs over all of the other ones?

_____

_____

_____

_____

_____

Name _____ Date _____

147. There are a lot of wild and crazy stunts you can do in this world. Skydiving, bungee jumping and ski jumping are just a few of the things people do when they're seeking thrills. If you were looking for a thrill, what activities do you think you would do? Who would you go with and how would you make sure you would end up safe?

_____

_____

_____

_____

148. We sometimes take for granted all of the things that our parents do for us, especially when it comes to things around the house. Imagine that you had to do all of the following in one day and write about how you'd handle it: cooking breakfast, lunch and dinner, washing dishes, making the bed, sweeping and vacuuming the floor, taking out the trash and doing laundry.

_____

_____

_____

_____

Name _____ Date _____

149. In lots of science fiction, the characters travel in a giant space
ship from planet to planet, meeting with aliens and exploring the universe. In the future,
this sort of space travel might actually be possible. Pretend that you are travelling in one of
these ships and you come upon a race of aliens! What happens next?

_____

_____

_____

_____

150. When you were little, did you have a stuffed animal or a toy that you couldn't leave
home without? What did you like so much about that toy? What do you think of now when
you think of it?

_____

_____

_____

_____

Name _____ Date _____

151. What are some of the benefits that a kid has over a grownup?
Vice versa, what are some of the advantages being a grownup has over being a kid? Based on these benefits, do you think it's better being a kid or an adult?

_____

_____

_____

_____

_____

152. In the past, when something important happened, nobody would know about it until they read it in the newspaper. Later, the television news came along, usually a couple of times a day. Now there are news channels 24 hours a day and there are websites that update constantly. How do you think the world has changed now that news gets out so much more quickly?

_____

_____

_____

_____

Name _____ Date _____

153. One of the most unfair things in this world is when people start being prejudiced about the color of other people's skin. Important activists like Martin Luther King, Jr., Rosa Parks and Gandhi showed that people should be treated equally. What would you do if you saw someone being prejudiced and talking badly about a particular race or person because of their skin color?

_____

_____

_____

_____

154. While you are typically able to go to school and play at recess, there are some kids who are sick all of the time and as a result they have to stay at home or a hospital. What would it be like if you were constantly fighting a disease instead of playing outside? How would you keep your spirits up and who do you think your biggest supporters would be?

_____

_____

_____

_____

Name _____ Date _____

155. While we constantly have things like refrigerated food, electrical power and clean running water, this is not the case throughout the entire world. Some people have to live in shacks with none of these things. What do you think it would be like to live in such places? What would you do to stay happy and healthy?

_____

_____

_____

_____

_____

156. At some points during American history, there was a thing called a draft. The draft meant that anyone over the age of 18 had a chance to be picked for military service, even if they didn't want to go. There are multiple countries that still have a draft or a requirement to serve in the military like Israel. What do you think it would be like if you were forced to go into the Army?

_____

_____

_____

_____

_____

Name _____ Date _____

157. Your parents do not always have it easy, trying to make sure you and your family have good food on the table and that you are able to do things in the future like go to college and be happy. What are 10 things that you could do for your parents to make their lives better and how do you think those things would help?

_____

_____

_____

_____

_____

158. One of the most embarrassing things that can happen when you're a kid is when you have a crush on someone and the secret gets out before you're ready to tell that person. Imagine that your biggest crush has come up to you telling that he or she has heard the rumor. How do you respond?

_____

_____

_____

_____

_____

Name _____ Date _____

159. The winter holidays are a wonderful time of year for most people as they get to spend time with family and friends and receive presents. Keep in mind though; there are people who have to spend their holiday alone, like those at homes for the elderly with no family. Write a little card to a stranger who lives in one of these places for the holidays to keep up their holiday cheer.

_____

_____

_____

_____

_____

160. Some of the most interesting people in the world decide from an early age to dedicate their lives to a major cause like ending world hunger or saving the rainforest. If you had to choose a cause for yourself, what do you think it would be? What are at least three things you can do right now that would go toward your major goal?

_____

_____

_____

_____

_____

Name _____ Date _____

161. People say that you pass by a thousand different stories a day, as almost every person that you walk by has a story of his own. Create a story about a random person that you passed by today or someone in the room. If the person seemed grumpy, create a story of why he was grumpy. If he seemed happy, explain why. Go into extreme detail.

_____

_____

_____

_____

_____

162. What is the most memorable dream or nightmare that you have ever had? Go into detail about it and why it has stuck with you. Imagine that you could go into that dream or nightmare and have full control over it. How would it have changed?

_____

_____

_____

_____

_____

Name _____ Date _____

163. Describe the place that you and your family live. How many
rooms are there? What is the color of the outside and the walls on the inside? Write all about your house, your neighborhood and your room. Talk about the things you like about it and the things you don't.

_____

_____

_____

_____

_____

164. A popular phrase for parents to say when they're scolding you is "when I was your age…" What do you think your parents were like when they were your age? How did they act and were they really the good kids that they claim to be?

_____

_____

_____

_____

Name _____ Date _____

165. While giving money to charity is a great way to help out, another thing you can do is give your time. What are some of the things in your area you could give your time volunteering for? Why would you choose those things and who would they benefit?

_____

_____

_____

_____

166. Some of us are lucky enough to have a favorite pet in our house like a dog, cat or fish. Recount a day in the life of your pet from his perspective. Imagine that the pet speaks in English and can talk about everything that happened to him at great length.

_____

_____

_____

_____

Name _____ Date _____

167. Talking on the phone can make some people feel nervous. Are
you one of those people that feel nervous on the phone or are you more confident? If you
are nervous, what are some of the things you think you could do to feel less nervous?

_____

_____

_____

_____

168. While a lot of horror movies portray zombies, vampires and other monsters as being
scary, what if they actually did exist and they weren't so bad after all? Imagine that you
have sat down to chat with a zombie, a vampire and a werewolf at a coffee shop. What do
you all talk about?

_____

_____

_____

_____

Name _____ Date _____

169. Imagine that a friend told you the biggest secret you'd ever
heard in your life. Do you think that you'd be able to keep it or that it would be too tough?
If you did tell somebody, who would you tell and why?

_____

_____

_____

_____

170. You and your friends have decided to play a giant game of Capture the Flag
throughout an entire park. Who are some of the people on your team and who are some of
the people on the other team? Describe the game, how it goes and who wins!

_____

_____

_____

_____

Name _____ Date _____

171. What is your favorite game that you like to play? Is it something with other people or a game that you play alone? Who would be the best people to play it with and where would you play it?

_____

_____

_____

_____

172. Talk about a time in which you felt very proud of yourself. What did you do and why did you do it? Did you receive any awards for doing this task?

_____

_____

_____

_____

Name _____ Date _____

173. Ten years from now what do you think the world will be like?
How will things have changed and how would they change for you (you will be in your first year of college by then!)?

_____

_____

_____

_____

174. What is the best birthday party you've ever been to and why? What was the theme of the party and what did you bring as a gift (and if it was your own party, what did you get as a gift)?

_____

_____

_____

_____

Name _____ Date _____

175. What is your favorite movie of all time? Why is it so good? Do you remember who you were with the first time that you saw it?

_____

_____

_____

_____

_____

176. What would you do if you were the President of the United States? How would you help people and how would you change things about the world?

_____

_____

_____

_____

_____

Name _____ Date _____

177. Talk about a time that you were on a plane. What did you see when you looked out of the window? Where were you going? Do you remember if there was anything special happening on the plane itself?

_____

_____

_____

_____

178. What is the best meal that you've ever had? Who cooked it and why do you remember it so well? Do you think that you'd be able to cook the same thing if you had the chance?

_____

_____

_____

_____

Name _____ Date _____

179. What would you do with a million dollars? What would you
buy? Would you give any of it away to charity? Which charity would you give some to?

_____

_____

_____

_____

_____

180. What is the most memorable dream or nightmare that you've ever had? Describe the
dream from the beginning to the end and try not to leave out any details.

_____

_____

_____

_____

_____

Name _____ Date _____

181. If you had your choice of living anywhere in the world where
would it be? Why would you live there and what do you think would change about your
life?

_____

_____

_____

_____

182. Some people have the tradition of sending a letter to all of their family members
reporting on some of the major events of the year. Write a letter recounting the major good
and bad things that have happened to you that your family might be interested in hearing.

_____

_____

_____

_____

Name _____ Date _____

183. There are those who believe in Santa Claus and those who absolutely don't. Imagine and construct a debate between two children who think differently on the issue. Who wins the debate and why?

_____

_____

_____

_____

184. Christmas is typically associated with cold weather and occasionally even snow. How would Christmas be different for you and your family if you were instead on a tropical island during the occasion? Write a detailed story about the situation.

_____

_____

_____

_____

Name _____ Date _____

185. Hallmark and other greeting card companies save some of their best poetry and sayings for their Christmas cards. Create several poems that would work well in greeting cards for the holiday season. They can be serious, funny, silly or any other tone you'd like.

_____

_____

_____

_____

_____

186. As your parents put the finishing touches on the final light in their massive from yard display, a circuit shorts and knocks out all of the power on your block for Christmas Eve. Write a story about what happens next.

_____

_____

_____

_____

Name _____ Date _____

187. Write a story for a sequel to one of your favorite Christmas movies. Include which characters will be returning, the new ones that will be introduced and where the story will be set.

_____

_____

_____

_____

188. There are several new adaptations about Hanukkah, such as the Hanukkah bush, an assimilation of the Christmas tree. There have also been stories about someone named Hanukkah Harry, who is a parody of Santa Claus. Create a silly story about Hanukkah Harry and how he fits into the holiday.

_____

_____

_____

_____

Name _____ Date _____

189. The menorah is the major symbol of the miracle of Hanukkah
and it demonstrates how the small amount of oil was able to light the holy temple for eight
whole nights. Have you ever had something last much longer than you expected it to? How
grateful were you that it lasted so long?

_____

_____

_____

_____

190. The Hebrew letters on the spinning toy, the dreidel, translate either into "a great
miracle happened there" (for those outside of Israel) or "a great miracle happened here"
(for those in Israel). Have you ever seen a great miracle in your life? If you did, how would
you commemorate the occasion?

_____

_____

_____

_____

Name _____ Date _____

191. You are standing on the edge of the sand right before your feet will hit the water. You stare out into the ocean. Write a story about the many thoughts going through your head.

_____

_____

_____

_____

192. Write a story about a child building a sand castle and talking through the entire story of the medieval town he is creating. The king, the queen, the knights, and all the people inside are given personalities and back stories. Be as detailed as possible.

_____

_____

_____

_____

Name _____ Date _____

193. Imagine that you are a crab walking along on the ocean floor,
trying to avoid all of the people while trying to get a bit of food from every passerby. It is a
complicated job. Talk about a day in the life of Herbert J. Crab (or whatever your name is).

_____

_____

_____

_____

_____

194. Talk about a sport that you've played on the beach, whether a simple game of catch or
some kind of water football hybrid. Who did you play with and how did the game go? If
you've never done this, make up a story about it.

_____

_____

_____

_____

_____

Name _____ Date _____

195. What is the most beautiful beach that you've ever been to?
Describe the entire scene thoroughly and explain why the beach was such a pretty sight to behold. If you have never been to an aesthetically pleasing beach, create a story in which you had.

_____

_____

_____

_____

196. What would be your perfect beach day? Describe the weather and the people you would be going with? Who would you see there and what activities would be occurring during your perfect stay?

_____

_____

_____

_____

Name _____ Date _____

197. Write about eating an entire bowl of fruit. Feel free to make the
fruits as exotic and interesting as possible. Really play on the use of all five senses with
this exercise.

_____

_____

_____

_____

_____

198. Your good friend has invited you over for pretty much the worst smelling and tasting
meal you've ever experienced. Describe the entire encounter including every stomach
churning bite.

_____

_____

_____

_____

_____

Name _____ Date _____

199. You have been roped into cooking for 100 people! Describe
your day from the trip to the supermarket all the way through to the interminable clean up.

_____

_____

_____

_____

_____

200. Though the book *Cloudy with a Chance of Meatballs* is fiction...giant portions of food
begin raining down from the sky! How do you spend your first week in this new world
where hunger is a memory and umbrellas are a necessity?

_____

_____

_____

_____

_____

Extra Page

Name _____ Date _____

_____

_____

_____

_____

_____

_____

_____

_____

_____

_____

ABOUT THE AUTHOR

Bryan Cohen is a writer, actor and director who grew up in Dresher, Pennsylvania just outside of Philadelphia. He graduated from the University of North Carolina at Chapel Hill with degrees in English and Dramatic Art along with a minor in Creative Writing. His books on writing prompts and writing motivation have sold over 10,000 copies and they include *1,000 Creative Writing Prompts: Ideas for Blogs, Scripts, Stories and More*, *1,000 Character Writing Prompts: Villains, Heroes and Hams for Scripts, Stories and More*, *500 Writing Prompts for Kids: First Grade through Fifth Grade*, *1,000 Character Writing Prompts: Villains, Heroes and Hams for Scripts, Stories and More* and *The Post-College Guide to Happiness*. Cohen continues to produce and perform plays and films in between his books and freelance writing work. He lives in Chicago.

Made in the USA
Lexington, KY
12 January 2013